The
SENIOR CITIZENS'
SURVIVAL GUIDE

The

SENIOR CITIZENS' SURVIVAL GUIDE

Bob Feigel
and
Malcolm Walker

MAINSTREAM
PUBLISHING

Concept and text: Bob Feigel
Artist: Malcolm Walker

© Copyright 1988 SeTo Publishing

This edition published in 1989 by
Mainstream Publishing (Edinburgh) Ltd
7 Albany Street, Edinburgh
EH1 3UG

British Library Cataloguing in Publication data
Feigel, Bob
     The senior citizens survival guide
     1. English humorous cartoons — Collections from individual artists
     1. Title 11. Walker, Malcolm
     741. 5'942

     ISBN 1-85158-246-0

Printed in Hong Kong by Colorcraft Ltd.

Senior Citizen: (ˈsiːnjə ˈsitizen) adj.,n
Anyone over 55 who still thinks life is worth living.

a sophisticated self-defence technique

INTRODUCTION

The Senior Citizen

In enlightened societies, Senior Citizens are venerated.

They are placed high upon pedestals of honour and respect.

They are listened to by their children and their children's children. Each word, each opinion cherished as a priceless pearl of wisdom.

Senior Citizens are treasured in their Golden Years. Pampered through the Autumn of their lives. Not only that, but their wishes are carried out before they are!

In enlightened societies, the older you get, the better IT gets.

Unfortunately, unless you understand   and eat with chopsticks forget it.

A Raw Deal

So, what's it like being a Senior Citizen in today's unenlightened western society? How about bleak?

After all, you've spent a lifetime working, paying taxes, playing by the rules. And now, just when your investment should start paying dividends, you're turfed out ... banished. Exiled to geriatric ghettos for the grey.

Suddenly no one is listening. Years of experience mean nothing. Your opinions don't count. You've been sentenced to an almost ghost-like existence on the sidelines of society.

No doubt about it — you're getting a raw deal.

Fighting back

Then why not retaliate? Get even? Fight back and change this rotten, superficial, youth-oriented culture and transform it into an enlightened society where you don't have to eat with chopsticks.

But first you have to survive and this little handbook can help you do it.

PART I – SURVIVAL SKILLS

SHOPLIFTING FOR BEGINNERS
Introduction
Basic Rules
Child In Pram Ruse

CREATIVE COOKING WITH PET FOODS
Introduction
You Are What You Eat
Memorable Meals
Our Chef Suggests . . .
Sample Recipe
Entertaining for the Impoverished

GLAMOUR FOR GERIATRICS
Introduction
Do-It-Yourself Face-Lifts
Staying In Style
Salvation Army Fashion Supplement
   (Includes Health Warning)

SELF DEFENCE
The Problem
The Solution
Weapons
Two Ways To Maim With A Crutch
Diversions
Home Protection
Group Tactics

SHOPLIFTING FOR BEGINNERS

In view of today's economy, shoplifting should be thought of as a self-help programme designed to give Senior Citizens a practical alternative to starving. But there are rules . . .

Basic Rules

DON'T FEEL GUILTY

If you're going to feel guilty, you might as well skip this section and go straight to Creative Cooking With Pet Foods.

DON'T BE GREEDY

Be selective. Use this practical survival skill to supplement basics like bread and water, with the prohibitively expensive luxuries like meat, cheese, butter, coffee, soap and laxatives.

DON'T BE OBVIOUS

Try not to draw attention to yourself. Better still, work in pairs and get a confederate to create a timely diversion while you hobble into action.

don't be greedy

Like any other professional skill, shoplifting requires patience and practice. So if at first you don't succeed, try, try, try again.

shoplifting: wrong

shoplifting: right

We Recommend . . .

THE CHILD IN PRAM RUSE

Borrow a child who's still young enough to burble incoherently. Borrow a pram to put it in. If you can get paid for babysitting at the same time, so much the better!

Grab one of those hand-held shopping baskets on the way into the supermarket and fill it with unwanted basics while stuffing expensive luxury items underneath the child.

As you approach the checkout counter, casually lean down to the child and firmly pinch one of its pudgy little thighs. Use a hat pin if you prefer.

Appear concerned but helpless as the child errupts into a fit of mega-decibel rage which drives everyone around you bonkers.

Should the child show any sign of calming down, pinch, tweak or stick it again and again so that it is screaming bloody murder by the time you reach the checkout counter.

Apologise profusely to the checkout operator, dump your basket of basics on the counter and head quickly for the nearest exit.

Everyone will be so delighted to see both of you go that no one will think to search the pram.

appear confused but helpless

look upon shoplifting as an adventure, and remember Robin Hood

CREATIVE COOKING WITH PET FOODS

You have probably noticed that pet foods are really catching on with Senior Citizens these days.

Why?

Why not! Pet foods are packed with protein and are a great source of fibre. They are convenient, versatile and easy to use.

So why waste them on pets?

You Are What You Eat

Poverty aside, pet foods have become nutritionally superior to most people foods.
Compare the labels:
Why doesn't Chef Waldo tell you about vitamins, minerals, protein or calories?
What is Chef Waldo trying to hide?!?

Dehydrated leftover vegetables, non-fat milk solids, various spices, assorted flavourings, culinary extracts, stabilizer, preservatives, thickeners, colouring, acid regulators, emulsifier, anti-coagulant, anti-regurgitators, non-specified meat chunks, bits, pieces, stuff, things, sugar, salt, MSG.

which would YOU rather eat?

Memorable Meals

Combine your favourite recipes with a variety of pet foods for a series of memorable meals in a jiffy. Replace outrageously expensive meat and fish with wholesome, value packed pet foods today!

Our chef suggests . . .

HEALTHY BREAKFASTS
Doggie Biscutts & Laying Mash Muesli
Gro-Pup Granola

LIGHT LUNCHES
Go-Cat Tuna Salad
Jellymeat Mousse
Pal Liver Paté
Rabbit Mix Rissoles (vegetarian)
Gourmet Pet Roll Paté
Chum Croquettes Rolled in
Billy Peach Silver Sand

HEARTY MAINS
Fido Meat Loaf
Gravy Train Goulash
Meaty Bites Stew

SUCCULENT SEAFOODS
Meow Bouillabaisse
Biscat Bisque
Sardines in Aspic on Toast

ETHNIC DELIGHTS
Mexican: Chilli Con Kiblex
American: Fidoburgers; Tuxettes Texas Style
Chinese: Sweet 'n' Sour Jellychicken;
Jellyfish & Cashews
Japanese: Meow Sardine Sushi;
Tucker Box Teriaki

DELICIOUS DESERTS
Doggie Bon-Bons & Ice Cream
Budgie Seed Balls in Chocolate Sauce

Sample Recipe

MEAT LOAF AU FIDO
The beauty of cooking with pet foods is that most of the ingredients are already included.

For this moist and meaty Loaf, all you need is:
three large cans of Fido dog food
one large onion
one tbs cooking oil
a deep, loaf-shaped 'non-stick' baking pan.

1) Empty contents of Fido cans into large mixing bowl.
2) Gently sauté onion in oil.
3) Mix sautéed onion with Fido in mixing bowl.
4) Chuck the whole lot into the baking pan.
5) Place in oven on medium heat for 10 mins.

Serves 4 adults, 6 midgets, or 1 teenager.

gently sautéed to perfection

Entertaining for the Impoverished

If the high cost of entertaining is all that's keeping you from throwing a gala dinner party then have a look at this.

Apéritif — '*Attila*' After Shave (You can find countless unused bottles of this uniquely aromatic fluid at the local rubbish dump shortly after Father's Day).

Main Course — Assorted vegetables, freshly selected from your grocer's rubbish, and Garfield Creme of Chicken on Rice (Shoplifted).

House Wine — Raspberry Kool-Aid in methylated spirits (shoplifted).

Dessert — Ten milligram tabs of Valium, suspended in Lime jelly and eaten with chopsticks

NB — Should a meatier main course be desired, get in the habit of setting traps for small animals or neighbourhood pets.

GLAMOUR HINTS FOR GERIATRICS

Growing old feels bad enough without having to look the part
as well. But thanks to modern cosmetic surgery, you can
fold back the years, tuck away the ravages of time,
and look young again.
At least, from the neck up!

Do-It-Yourself Face Lifts
Unfortunately cosmetic surgery has become so expensive
that Senior Citizens are resorting to do-it-yourself
face lifting.
Despite obvious drawbacks, all you need are some
helping hands, a firm grip and a little imagination.

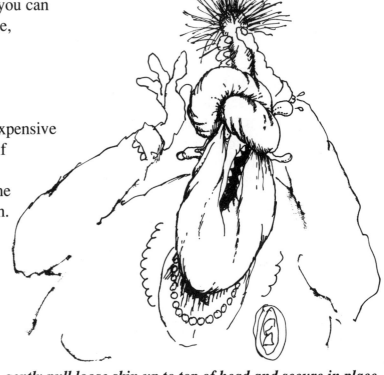

gently pull loose skin up to top of head and secure in place,
camouflage with large hat, wig or well-gelled mohawk haircut

always take care to ensure that your old body can keep up with your new face

Staying In Style.

Just because you are old and impoverished doesn't mean you can't dress in style.
Maybe not this year's style. Maybe not even last year's style. But at least some year's
style! So check out your local second-hand clothing shop.

After all, the clothes you gave away to charity twenty years ago are probably this
season's *haute couture*.

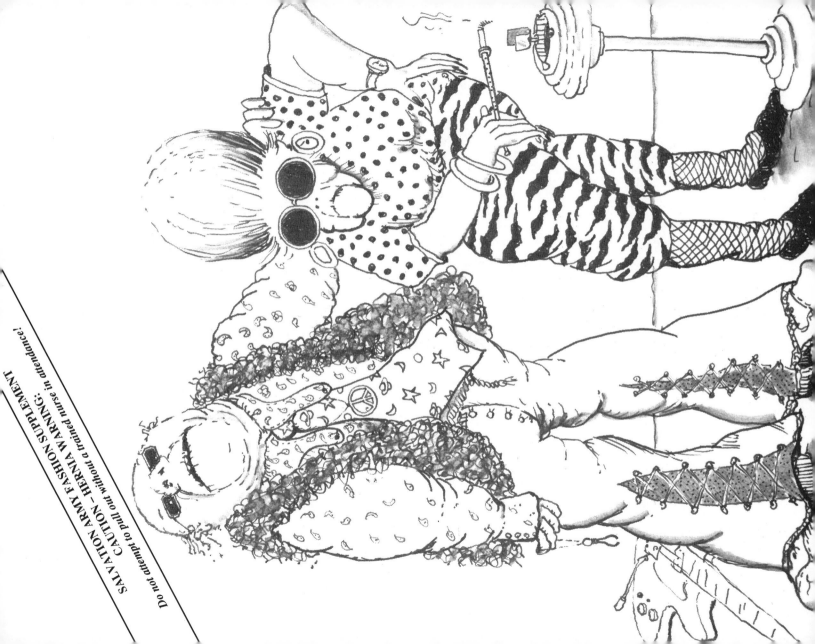

SELF DEFENCE

The Problem

Being a Senior Citizen these days is worse than being on the 'Endangered Species' list. Not only do you stand a good chance of being mugged, burgled or purse-snatched, you're fair game for every human parasite from con men to tax men. Sad to say, today's society dismisses Senior Citizens as an obsolete minority group not worth protecting. Worse, they see you as a hopeless group of decaying old has-beens on automatic self-destruct (For more 'insulting terms' see glossary).

The Solution

FIGHT BACK!

So what if you're a bit rusty and worn out. So what if you can't fight with your fists. You're still a long way from being that doddering, moth-eaten old fossil they think you are. (For even more insulting terms, try the same glossary).

Even if you can't outrun 'em, you can outsmart 'em. Besides, who would expect a helpless, crumbling old relic like you to use sophisticated self-defence techniques like these?

Weapons

CANES AND SWORD STICKS

The trouble with these 'traditional' weapons is that bludgeoning takes up too much energy and punctured arteries are *so* messy.

CAMERA FLASH

A small pocket camera with a built-in flash is perfect for causing temporary blindness, giving you the chance to apply your heavy, steel-capped walking shoes to the soft spots of a body. This was good enough for James Stewart in Hitchcock's 'Rear Window', remember.

UMBRELLAS

The metal tips on some models can be sharpened to a lethal point, and an automatic umbrella shoved firmly down an assailant's throat and triggered can cause extreme discomfort.

PENSION BOOKS

Say you're being menaced by some great hulking thug and all you've got to defend yourself with is a pension book.

No problem. Simply roll the book up as tightly as possible and shove it into your assailants eye, throat or solar plexus.

If this doesn't work, let attacker read it — he may feel so sorry for your fixed income level that he will press a few coins into your hand and go away.

PILLS

If the odds are stacked against you and you have to run away, this little trick can save your life.

Get as far ahead of your pursuer as possible and spill your bottle of pills directly in his path.

He'll either slip on them and fall down, injuring himself in the process, or he'll give up the chase in disgust at this pitiful gesture of defence.

NB — don't use the last of your heart pills for this!

Two Ways To Maim With A Crutch

Killing with a crutch is easy. It's maiming that takes skill.

First, determine if you need crutches to keep upright. If so, use only one at a time or you'll fall down.

CAUTION: DO NOT ATTEMPT THESE TECHNIQUES ON STAIRS, MOVING ESCALATORS OR WAXED FLOORS.

THE ONE-CRUTCH CRUTCH CRUNCHER

Wait until your assailant is within striking distance, then suddenly look beyond him so that he thinks someone is coming up from behind.

As he turns to look, bring left crutch right up between his legs with enough force to lift him to his toes. This will cause him great pain followed by intense agony.

Take advantage of this moment to smash him over the back of the head and limp away, fastish.

the old 'one . . .

. . . two'

THE TWO-CRUTCH PINCER
Judge your assailant's distance. Look him straight in the eye.
Aim for the neck. Thrust with your right crutch, follow through with your left, and pinch until he loses consciousness.

Diversions

BLINDNESS

For this scam, you'll need mirrored sunglasses, steel-toed footwear, and a white cane tipped with lead.

Thinking that you are easy pickings, a mugger will approach more openly as you shuffle and tap your way through the rougher parts of town.

Using your cane, 'feel' your way towards your mugger and tap around his feet. Stop, do your Stevie Wonder act, and say in a quavering voice "Is anybody there?"

This will appeal to the mugger's perverted sense of humour, and give you the chance to kick him on the shin with your steel-toed carpet slipper.

As he's hopping around, remember that this trick will work only once, so quickly decide which part of his body to break with your lead-weighted cane.

. . . with your steel-toed carpet slipper

PALSY

As a delaying tactic, feigning palsy requires more co-ordination than acting skill, and can be very useful in a one-to-one confrontation.

First, make sure you carry a sock filled with sand down your trousers/skirt, and a pocketful of loose change.

When accosted and asked for money, start shaking and fish out a handful of change. Offer it to your attacker, shaking so hard it all falls to the ground at his feet.

As your assailant bends down to pick it up, whip out the sock full of sand and put him away.

Home Protection

GRANDCHILDREN, USE OF

When it comes to laying booby-traps, grandchildren are indispensible.

Pick a room nearest to the most obvious burglar entry point to your home. Buy lots of toys, marbles, roller skates, lego, etc., and invite your grandchildren or neighbour's children over to play. Throw them out after half an hour, that will be enough. Ask them to be sure and tidy up before they go. Then close up the room and never invite them back. Any burglar entering this room is history.

SPRAY PAINT CANS

Here is the perfect weapon to use on children. Always shake the can before opening the door, or paying a visit to your grandchildren.

hi, Grandad!

FEAR

Instead of a traditional security system that sounds an alarm which everyone, including the police, ignores, install one which turns on a tape recorder with this message —

"Welcome to the home of Don 'Vicious' Vincente, recently retired Godfather of the local Family. The Don is sorry he has missed you, but he is out visiting the surviving relatives of the last person who entered his house without permission.
Please do not leave a message, as hidden cameras have already recorded your identity. Have a nice day."

Group Tactics

Unless you're a confirmed masochist, or are contemplating suicide, any foray into enemy territory should be planned with military precision.

Send out a suitable decoy to lull the enemy into a sense of false security, then . . .

a suitable decoy

. . . spring a trap which will make Custer's Last Stand look like a tea party.

vigilantes in action

PART II – SOCIAL SKILLS

REVENGE, SWEET REVENGE
Annoying Your Children
Embarrassing Them
Worrying Them
Making Them Feel Guilty

OUT TO PASTURE
Introduction
The Right Spot
Combatting Boredom

SENILITY AS A CON
Shopping
Public Transport
Eating Out

SOME ADVANTAGES IN BEING OLD

THE LAST LAUGH
Introduction
Adventures In Euthanasia
Cremations — Going Out With A Bang
The Last Word
On The Cheap
Over The Top
Where There's A Will . . .

GLOSSARY OF INSULTING TERMS

Developing from a basic survivor into a sophisticated, finely-honed Social Activist is worth the effort, because it gives you a new lease on life.

Suddenly shackles fall, and the load lifts from shoulders too long stooped. Eyes brighten, sinews firm. The step quickens and blood, until recently coagulated in horrid little lumps like poorly-mixed custard, once again flows freely through your veins.

But there are tests ahead! Here's how to cope.

REVENGE, SWEET REVENGE

Whoever said that revenge isn't fun must have been a Junior Citizen. Besides, you might not get another chance.

Annoying Your Children
Annoying your offspring is easy — just do to them what they did to you while they were growing up.

PAY THEM A VISIT AND . . .
• take along all your dirty washing.
• go straight to the refrigerator, carefully study the contents, complain that there's nothing you like, then devour everything in sight.

devour everything in sight

- leave a mess in every room, and make sure you turn on all the lights.
- tie up the telephone for hours, making long-distance calls wherever possible.
- break a few of their favourite glasses.
- get up earlier than they do and use up all the milk/coffee/tea.
- switch on the TV then leave the room.
- crank up the volume on the stereo and insist you're hard of hearing when they ask you to turn it down.
- become suddenly infirm when asked to do anything around the house.
- borrow their car and return it with a near-empty fuel tank.
- come home without it and say that you can't remember where you left it.
- come for a week, stay for eight and pay for nothing.
- slam the door when you leave.

THE GOLDEN RULES

- borrow money, tools, clothes, etc., and never return them.
- call them collect from faraway places and ask them to send you the fare home.
- forget all their birthdays.
- phone them early Sunday morning, or during dinner or in the middle of their favourite TV show, and say you feel lonely and just thought you'd have a little chat.
- encourage your grandchildren to do all the rotten things their parents did at their age.
- never miss a chance to tell them that they just don't understand what its like to be your age.

encourage your grandchildren to do what their parents did . . .

Embarrassing Them

• dress in your best clothes and turn up at your son/daughter's place of work when you are sure he/she is away. Proudly tell everyone in sight that it's your birthday and you are being taken out to lunch. When someone explains that your offspring isn't there, say "Oh! Seems I've been forgotten again . . ." and shuffle sadly away.

• surprise them at their next pool or spa party by jumping in nude.

jump in nude

• pretend to be a vegetarian at their next barbeque and harrass all their meat eating guests.

• dance at their wedding.

• gate-crash their next office party and make a pass at their boss/boss's wife.

Or show up at their next important dinner party, dressed in your grubbiest gardening clothes, and beg for food.

beg for food

Worrying Them

Should you have any second thoughts about worrying your children, simply cast your mind back to those sleepless nights, missed meals and grey hairs. Here are a few useful phrases:

It's not too late to change my will.

You know, it's about time I thought about getting married again.

We've always counted on spending our last days with you.

spending our last days with you . . .

What would you say about me joining one of those communes?

Wonder how much money we could spend before we die...?

And if none of the above work, take off on a two week's holiday and don't tell them.

Making Them Feel Guilty

Parents have been making their children feel guilty since the beginning of time, so why stop a good thing now? Here are some more useful phrases:

You wouldn't dare talk like that if your father was still alive.

Your mother would turn in her grave if she heard you speaking to me like that.

How can you say that, after all I've done for you?

And to think what I've sacrificed for YOU!

Don't worry about me. You have your own life to live (accompanied by sigh).

I guess I'm just no good for anything any more.

You won't have me to push around much longer.

I could shrivel up and die for all you care.

You'll miss me when I'm gone.

At least my cat loves me.

out to pasture

OUT TO PASTURE

In some societies, Senior Citizens are expected to spend the last years of their lives living in the comfort of the Family home, surrounded by their children, grandchildren and great-grandchildren.

In others, old people are more or less expected to walk out into the wilderness and die alone.

With a choice like that, maybe Retirement Communities aren't such a bad idea after all?

Choosing The Right Spot

Whether it's a huge community of several thousand, or a smaller, more intimate little retirement village, it is a good idea to check it out carefully before signing on the dotted line. Some rules to follow.

Don't involve your children.
*They don't have to live there, but **you** do . . .*

Pretend to be checking the place out for YOUR parents.
*Get an idea of what you can **really** expect.*

note: if you get a chance, check out the Matron's arms for strange tattoos.
You can never be too careful!

After the official tour by the Superintendant, or Kommandant, or whoever fronts up as supremo, insist on 'a quiet hour' by yourselves, to 'get the feel of the place'. This gives you the chance to:

- cross-examine a few inmates.
- check out the kitchen cupboards for suspicious quantities of pet foods.
- take a sample of the water for analysis (some places put embalming fluid into the drinking water, to keep everyone looking younger).
- if applicable, invite yourself to the next meal and insist on eating what the residents eat.
  compare this to what the staff eat, and to what the residents are paying for it.
- inspect the records of the local ambulance service *be wary of an unusually high turnover rate.*

select your rest home carefully

50

Combatting Boredom

OK. You've chosen your retirement spot, and moved in. Now what?

Here are some suggestions to make sure that at least you're not bored to death:

• Home brew is not only a fascinating hobby, it can make you many friends. Start with lagers and stouts, and graduate to your own still. Bathtub gin will ensure your popularity.

• Infiltrate the local Bridge Club and introduce a porn video night.

• Set up a gambling ring that takes bets on who's going to kick the bucket next. (No cheating.)

• Invite local Peeping Toms to start a neighbourhood-watch group.

• Organise practical adult education classes, like 'Do-It-Yourself Casket Making', 'Euthanasia For Beginners', or 'How to Con The Social Welfare Agencies'.

• Sabotage the speed governors on the golf carts.

SENILITY AS A CON

The nicest thing about taking advantage of your age is that you're only doing what young people expect, and therefore deserve.

Shopping

FASTER SHOPPING

Senior Citizens should not be expected to spend their Golden Years standing around in supermarkets, waiting to be checked-out.

Either go straight to the front of the line, barge in and pretend you're deaf should anyone complain, or push your fully laden trolley up to the '10 items or less' counter, ignoring all the dirty looks.

appear confused . . .

DISCOUNT SHOPPING

When asked to pay, appear confused when counting out your money, and put down less than required.

When the clerk points out your mistake, take all the money back and start again.

After a while the clerk will pay the difference just to get rid of you.

Public Transport

FREE BUS RIDES

Push to the front of the queue, using cane on shins where necessary. Get on first and stall the driver with small-talk and questions, while fumbling around pockets or purse for money.

Continue this routine until the folks behind you start grumbling at the driver, and someone — anyone — offers to pay your fare.

stretch out in comfort

NO STANDING

If all seats are full, limp painfully up to the nearest Junior Citizen, demand its seat, and wheeze directly into its face until it moves. When seated, start to tell the person next to you your life story, and soon you will be able to stretch out in comfort.

Eating Out
FREE LUNCH

Choose a decent restaurant. Enjoy an expensive meal. Walk out without paying.
If someone runs after you demanding payment, insist you've paid. . . you remember it clearly . . . or at least you think you do . . . but of course you do . . . you've never forgotten before . . . or at least you don't remember ever having forgotten before. . .
besides, here's the receipt (produce a bus ticket) . . . who put that there? . . . and so on . . .
Considering what it's costing this person to listen to such drivel, there will eventually come a time when it becomes uneconomic and you're left to digest your meal in peace.

SOME ADVANTAGES IN BEING OLD

• Meals on Wheels ladies flirt with you.
• Buying a round of drinks down at the local pub gets cheaper as your friends die off.
• Underwear doesn't have to be changed so often.
• **No one tries to sell you life insurance any more.**

Another is that religious nuts don't try as hard to recruit you, although they are still happy to hit you up for donations.
Here are some tips on how to deal with these obnoxious hustlers.
• Ask for a receipt.
• Say you haven't seen their guru/leader since you served time together for fraud and are sorry to see he still hasn't gone straight.
• If they're an eastern cult, invite them to your next bible class.
• If they're 'bible bashers', invite them to a séance at the Theosophical Hall.
• If they're neither, tell them to bugger off!

tell them to bugger off

THE LAST LAUGH

You may not be able to avoid the inevitable, but with a little forethought, a smidgen of imagination, and a dollop of good old vindictive bile, you can make bloody sure that those you leave behind know damn well 'who got the last laugh!'.

The Way Out
ADVENTURES IN EUTHANASIA
The euthanasia we're talking about shouldn't be confused with the teenage religious movement in Singapore.

Arrange for a tour of your favourite Malt Whisky distillery, and at the appropriate moment, 'fall' into the vat of your choice. It should not be difficult to avoid rescuers.

Visit the newspaper you like / hate most. Wait until the final edition is rolling, then hurl yourself between the press's rollers — you really will make the front page!

Hire a hitman, and outsmart him as long as you can.

Tell a gang member how silly he looks.

Expire into a bath of casting resin and become the world's largest door stop.

Make an effort to out-Evil Knievel. Get out your old easy riding machine, head for the Grand Canyon, and let 'er rip.

Going Out With a Bang

With space at a premium these days, more and more people are opting for cremation. Besides, it could be good practice for your next stop!

BIG BANG
By the time anyone finds out you've stuffed your do-it-youself casket with high explosives, you'll be long gone.

CHINESE NEW YEAR

Insist on being decked out in a favourite suit or dress, previously lined with firecrackers.

FRESH AIR FAREWELL (or *Hire-A-Pyre*)

For that al fresco funeral, line up a couple of old Army buddies who, at the appropriate moment, will step forward with flame-throwers, and really see you out.

The Last Word

For the last word in burials, have a tape player secreted in your casket and get a friend to activate the remote control which activates your voice, just as the casket goes down . . .

On The Cheap

Inexpensive burials don't necessarily have to be in cardboard caskets, especially with a little forward planning — and a little help from your friends.

• Have yourself packed and anonymously shipped to the tax department. COD.

• Arrange for a friend to stuff you into a rubbish bag and put you out on the pavement on collection day.

Over The Top

Cheap funerals might not suit every body, so here's an expensive but memorable idea.

SHOW TIME

A Hollywood producer will be needed to work closely with an Archbishop on this extravaganza, as nothing less than a large cathedral will do.

After a suitably solemn introduction by his Bishopness, exotically clad dancers from Caesar's Palace, Las Vegas, will perform a choreographed version of your life.
This will be followed with a selection of your favourite songs sung by the Mormon Tabernacle Choir, accompanied by the London Philharmonic Orchestra under the *baton* of Mark Knopfler.
The eulogy will be delivered . . . with appropriate pauses . . . by Ronald Reagan, reading from a script prepared by Kurt Waldheim's PR man.
Your lead-lined, gold and silver encrusted casket will ride comfortably to your resting place in a custom built Masserati hearse, and will be buried with full military honours by surviving members of Anwar Sadat's bodyguard.

Your children will be sent the bill.

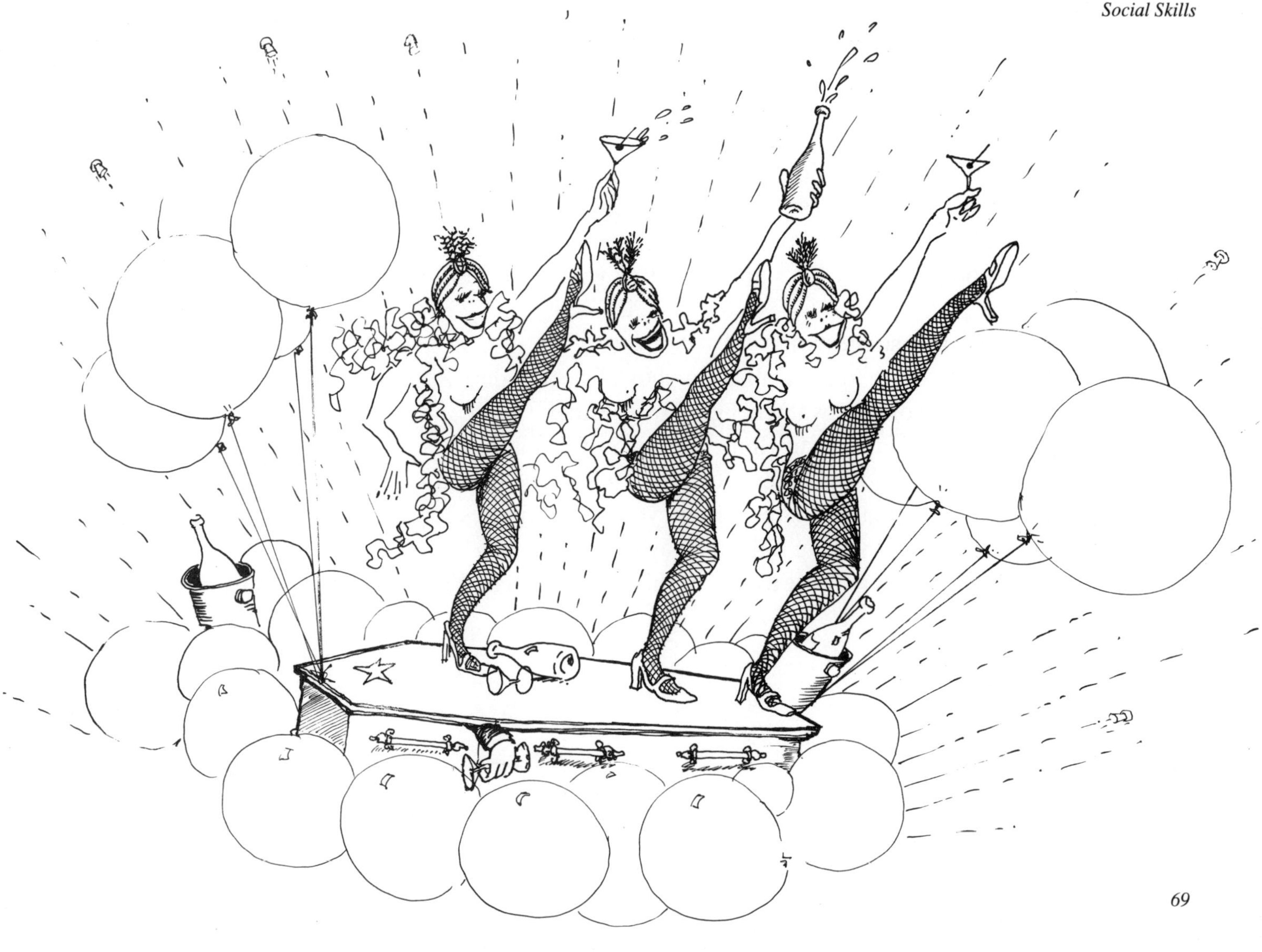

Where There's a Will . . .

This is definitely your last chance to hit 'em where it hurts.

Thanks to our near-inviolate legal system (made so through the dedicated avarice of lawyers) a properly attested Will is a thing of joy, a forever document.
Disputed over, argued about, killed for.
It is not only your Last Testament — It is your Last Test of Them!

Here are a few suggestions:
• leave everything to the Dallas Cowboys Cheerleaders Retirement Fund.
• or to the Arnold Schwarzenegger For President Fund.
• or to the Ronald Reagan Home for the Self Embalmed.
• or stick a pin into the Inner Mongolian telephone directory.
• or leave little treasure maps for everyone, with riddles for them to solve before they can find the loot you've hidden away over the years.
• **But don't forget to leave a copy of this book to each of your children. One day they will need it too.**

A WILL WITH A TWIST

Now that you've been laid to rest as per your wishes, you might as well have one more Last Laugh.

To ensure a large gathering of family, friends, business associates, neighbours, etc., have your lawyers invite everyone you've ever known to a large hall for the reading of your Will — suggesting they might learn 'something to their advantage'.

When they are all seated quietly, have your lawyer invite each guest to get up and say a few nice words about you. Each will be given a copy of a video you recorded before your passing, which your lawyer will then play on a large screen set up for the purpose. This is your last chance to say all the things you've ever wanted to say to various individuals in the audience; recommend that they enjoy the party afterwards, because all of your money went to pay for it.

GLOSSARY OF INSULTING TERMS

ancient old heap
at death's door
bag of bones
blue-rinse brigade
bumbling old twit
cantakerous old coot
crumbling
crusty old fart
decayed old fart
dingey as a wooden watch
doddering old twit
dotard
dusty
falling apart at the seams
fuddy-duddy
fusty
gone to seed
grey haired
had it
has-been
ineffectual old twerp
infirm
living on borrowed time

long-in-the-tooth
museum piece
moth eaten
mouldy oldy
no spring chicken
obsolete
old fogey
old fool
old fuss budget

old timer
oldy but mouldy
one foot in the grave
ornery old cuss
ossified old fossil
out of the Ark
over the hill
passé
past it
past your prime
rickety old geezer
ruin
rusty
shrivelled
silly old ding bat
stale
stubborn old goat
tiresome old geek
toothless relic
way past it
worm fodder
worn out
wrinklie

two insulting terms